Miss Kim and the Class

By Sue Dickson

Illustrated by Gwen Connelly

MODERN CURRICULUM PRESS

Pearson Learning Group

ISBN: 0-7652-3169-7

Printed in the United States of America.

5 6 7 8 9 10   07 06

Modern
Curriculum
Press

Pearson Learning Group

1-800-321-3106
www.pearsonlearning.com

Vocabulary Words
Short ĭ Words

1. Bill
2. bit
3. did
4. fix
5. gift
6. hit
7. in
8. it
9. Jill
10. Jim
11. kids
12. Kim

Vocabulary Words continued

13. Liz
14. milk
15. Miss
16. pick

17. pink
18. sip
19. sit
20. six

21. Tim
22. will
23. win

Review Words

24. at
25. bags
26. class
27. desk
28. egg

29. get
30. hand
31. led
32. left
33. mats

34. next
35. pen
36. pens
37. plant
38. set

Review Words continued

39. snack   42. have

40. snacks   43. is

41. tells

Story Words

44. good-bye   45. hello   46. pink

Miss Kim went in.
Miss Kim felt glad.

Miss Kim sat at the desk.

Bill went in.

Bill sat.
"Hello, Miss Kim," said Bill.

Jim and Will went in.

Jim and Will sat.
"Hello, Bill," said Jim.
"Hello, Bill," said Will.

Tim and Jill went in.

Tim and Jill sat.
Tim and Jill said, "Hello."

Liz went in.
Liz had a gift.

The gift is a red plant.

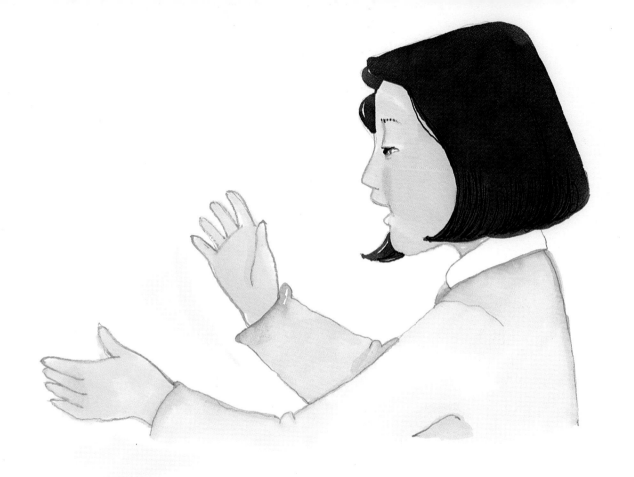

Miss Kim gets a red plant.

Miss Kim hit the plant.

The plant fell.

Miss Kim can fix the plant.

Liz will help Miss Kim.

Next, Liz sat.

The class had six kids.

Miss Kim led the class,
"E, e, egg."

The kids said, "E, e, egg."

Jim and Bill had red pens.
Liz had a red pen.

Tim and Will had red pens.
Jill had a pink pen.

The kids get the bags.

The kids sit.
The kids have snacks.

Liz had a snack.
Liz bit it.

Jill had a sip.
Jill can sip it.

Next, the kids get mats.

Six kids sit and rest.

The kids get set.

Miss Kim tells the kids,
"H, h, hand."

Will Jim win?

Will Miss Kim pick it?

Yes! Jim did win.

Jim will pick.
Jim is glad.

Will Jill get it?

Will Jill win?

Yes! Jill did win!

Jill will pick next.

The kids get set.

The kids get the bags.

Miss Kim helps the kids.

The kids get in.
The kids sit.

The kids left.
Good-bye!